Foods of
South Africa

Barbara Sheen

KIDHAVEN PRESS
A part of Gale, Cengage Learning

GALE
CENGAGE Learning·

Detroit • New York • San Francisco • New Haven, Conn • Waterville, Maine • London

© 2012 Gale, Cengage Learning

LIBRARY OF CONGRESS CATALOGING-IN-PUBLICATION DATA

Sheen, Barbara.
  Foods of South Africa / by Barbara Sheen.
    p. cm. -- (A taste of culture)
  Includes bibliographical references and index.
  ISBN 978-0-7377-5952-5 (hardcover)
  1. Cooking, South African--Juvenile literature. 2. Food--South Africa--Juvenile literature. 3. Cookbooks--Juvenile literature. 4. South Africa--Social life and customs--Juvenile literature. I. Title.
  TX725.S6S55 2012
  641.5968--dc23

                                                           2011039890

Kidhaven Press
27500 Drake Rd.
Farmington Hills MI 48331

ISBN-13: 978-0-7377-5952-5
ISBN-10: 0-7377-5952-6

Printed in the United States of America
1 2 3 4 5 6 7 15 14 13 12 11

Contents

Chapter 1

A Land of Contrasts

South Africa is a large country located on the southern tip of Africa. It is a land of contrasts. Within its borders are mountains, deserts, fertile valleys, grasslands, rivers, wetlands, coastal beaches, sub-Antarctic islands, diamond mines, wildlife parks, and bustling cities. Its people, too, are diverse. They represent many different cultural and ethnic groups. In fact, South Africa has eleven official languages. There are many different types of foods and recipes that are popular throughout the country, too. Essential ingredients such as corn, vegetables, seafood, and meat, which come from South African land and waters, are an important part of South African cooking.

FOOD REGIONS OF SOUTH AFRICA

ANGOLA

ZAMBIA

Lusaka ★

A F R I C A

Harare ★

ZIMBABWE

MOZAMBIQUE

Windhoek ★

BOTSWANA

NAMIBIA

Gaborone ★

Pretoria ★

Maputo ★

Mbabane ★

SWAZILAND

ATLANTIC OCEAN

SOUTH AFRICA

Bloemfontein ★

LESOTHO

Maseru ★

INDIAN OCEAN

Cape Town ★

| Cattle |
| Corn |
| Fish |
| Fruit |
| Grapes |
| Peanuts |
| Sheep |
| Sugar Cane |
| Vegetables |
| Wheat |

Mealies

Corn, or **mealie**, as it is known in South Africa, is South Africa's most important crop. In fact, corn is planted on half the farmland of South Africa. Corn also is exported to other countries, used in livestock feed, and is a main part of the South African people's diet.

South African corn is different from North American corn. The white or yellow kernels are larger and typically drier and less sweet than North American corn. As in North America, South Africans use corn in many ways. They fry unripe kernels in sunflower oil. They

Samp, which is made from dried corn, salt, and fat, is a popular side dish in South Africa.

Foods of South Africa

The Cradle of Humankind

Some of the oldest fossils and bones on the planet have been found near Johannesburg, South Africa. Scientists who study the remains of past cultures are called archaeologists. In South Africa, archaeologists have found human remains that date back more than 3 million years in dozens of caves. Among the most interesting finds are the remains of hominids, which are members of a family of primate mammals that walk on two feet, including humans and apes. Some scientists believe that the remains of now extinct hominids found in these caves were the ancestors of humans.

The remains of early humans dating back 1 million years have also been found in the caves, as well as evidence of early humans' first use of fire and stone tools. About 9,000 stone tools have been found in one cave alone. Because of these discoveries, the area has become known as the cradle of humankind.

grill corn on the cob. And, they turn dried corn kernels into **samp** (sahmp), a soft, puffy corn product that is also known as hominy. To make samp, South Africans soak corn kernels in hot water and a harsh chemical called lye. The lye causes the kernels to expand and split, leaving behind the soft insides. These are rinsed thoroughly to remove any traces of lye. Then they are dried in the sun and pounded into small pieces. These pieces are cooked in water with salt, fat, and sometimes beans. They are eaten as a side dish, like rice.

Crumbly Pap

Crumbly pap is not difficult to make. It can be topped with fried onions, tomatoes, and peppers or butter and plain yogurt. Spices can be added.

Ingredients
2 cups water
2 cups coarse yellow cornmeal
1 teaspoon salt
1 cup canned sweet corn, drained

Instructions
1. Bring the water to a boil.
2. Add the salt and cornmeal to the boiling water. Cover the pot. Reduce heat to low and cook for 5 minutes.
3. Stir the mixture. Cover the pot and cook for another 25 minutes.
4. Add the corn and stir the mixture. Cover the pot. Cook for 5 minutes more.

Serves 4–6.

Corn is also ground into cornmeal, or **mealie meal**. Mealie meal is used to make bread and, most importantly, it is turned into **pap**. Pap is a soft food similar to porridge that is made by boiling mealie meal in water. It has a plain, mild taste that goes well with both sweet and savory foods.

Depending on how much liquid is used, pap can be smooth and runny or thick and gritty. South African cooks create different dishes with pap depending on its consistency. Smooth, soft pap is much like oat-meal. It is eaten for breakfast when topped with milk, sugar, and peanut butter. Umphokoqo (oom-FOH-coh-coh), or crumbly pap, is popular for lunch and supper. Whether eaten cold and topped with sour milk or yogurt, or eaten hot and covered in milk, butter, and cheese, umphokoqo is a common light meal. It also is a favorite side dish when topped with tomato sauce. South Africans cannot get enough of it.

A blogger named Thuli recalls her childhood on a South African farm: "We ate umphokoqo on a daily basis. We had it for breakfast, lunch and supper. It was dished up in a big bowl and four children had to share two spoons. There was a big competition. You had to eat pretty fast and pass the spoons."[1]

Vegetable Soups, Stews, and Salads

In addition to corn, a variety of other vegetables play a big part in South African cooking. Some, like carrots, spinach, cabbage, pumpkins, and onions, are familiar to North Americans, while others are less so. Water-blommetjie (WAW-ter BLOOM-chee) is an example of a South African vegetable not commonly found in other parts of the world. It comes from a flower that can be eaten that grows wild along South African waterways. It tastes similar to asparagus, and is often an ingredient in South African stews.

Even those vegetables that are familiar to North Americans often look and taste much different in South Africa. For example, South African yams are not much

Sambal is a chunky, spicy condiment made from chili peppers, vegetables, and vinegar that is used as a dip or to flavor sauces and stews.

like the sweet, orange-fleshed sweet potatoes that are called yams in America. South African yams have yellow flesh and taste more like traditional potatoes.

South African cooks use these and other vegetables in soups, stews, and salads. They make them into fritters, savory puddings, and sauces. They also pickle them. Before refrigerators were available, South Africans pickled vegetables in order to keep them from spoiling. South Africans no longer have to worry about preserving their food in this way, yet they still enjoy eating pickled vegetables. In fact, pickled cucumbers, beets, and onions are all popular side dishes. Pickled unripe fruits are also enjoyed.

Pickled and fresh vegetables and fruit are key in-

Tomato-and-Onion Salad

This is a popular side dish. Soaking the onion in cold water makes the onion taste less bitter.

Ingredients

1 large tomato, thinly sliced
1 medium onion, thinly sliced
2 tablespoons red wine vinegar
½ teaspoon sugar
½ teaspoon salt

Instructions

1. Soak the onion slices in a bowl of ice water for ten minutes.
2. Mix together the vinegar, sugar, and salt.
3. Put the tomato and onion slices in a bowl. Gently toss together. Top with the vinegar mixture. (The mixture will not cover it like dressing. It is there to add flavor.)
4. Cover and refrigerate for one hour.

Serves 4.

Tomato and onion salad is a simple but tasty side dish.

gredients in chutney and sambal (SAHM-bahl). These are two relish-like condiments that are often served at meals. There are many varieties of both chutney and sambal. Sambal is chunky and spicy. It usually contains chili peppers, mixed vegetables, and vinegar. It is similar to Mexican salsa. Chutney looks like preserves and is thick and spreadable. Typically chutney is made with a single vegetable or fruit that is added to onions, vinegar, and sugar. Red- or green-tomato chutney, green-chili chutney, and apricot chutney are all favorites. South Africans slather chutney on meat the same way North Americans spread ketchup or mustard. They add sambal to sauces and stews, and they dip food in it, too. Both relishes add a sweet, zesty flavor to South African dishes.

Fish and Other Seafood

Fish and shellfish are other important foods in South Africa. The country has 1,739 miles (2,798km) of coastline on the Atlantic and Indian Oceans. Therefore, fishing has become an important industry. About 700,000 tons (635,000 metric tons) of fish are caught in South African waters each year. Tuna, cod, oysters, sardines, shrimp, trout, anchovies, lobsters, and **snoek** (snew) are just a few of the many different creatures that live in South African waters.

Snoek, in particular, is a local favorite. It is a barracuda-like fish with a rich flavor and oily texture. South Africans grill, broil, barbecue, and fry snoek. They wrap it in banana leaves and steam it over hot coals.

A woman grills freshly caught snoek, a fish that is popular among South Africans, particularly along the country's southwestern coast.

They cover it with spicy sauces and cook it in soups and stews. And, to preserve it, they salt, pickle, smoke, or dry it. Authors Magdaleen Van Wyk and Pat Barton explain: "The southwestern coast of the Cape [of Good Hope] is the world of salted and dried fish. If you drive along the coastal road … you will see butterflied whole snoek [fish that are slit open with the heads removed] … hanging out to dry on stands erected alongside sun washed windswept bays."[2]

Pickled fish are eaten often, too. Fish is pickled in vinegar and spices. Depending on what method the cook uses, pickled fish can taste sour, salty, spicy, and/or sweet. According to South African chef Michael Olivier, "Few Cape homes would not have their own

Fast Facts About South Africa

South Africa is bordered by the Atlantic and Indian Oceans and the nations of Namibia, Botswana, Swaziland, Mozambique, and Zimbabwe. The independent kingdom of Lesotho is located within South Africa's borders.

South Africa is about twice the size of Texas and has a mild climate. It is divided into nine provinces, which are much like U.S. states. Its capital is Pretoria. Its unit of money is the rand.

About 44.6 million people live in South Africa. These people come from 30 different ethnic groups. Seventy-seven percent are black Africans. South Africa has eleven official languages, including English, Zulu, Afrikaans, and Xhosa.

Diamond, gold, platinum, iron, and silver mining are important South African industries. Other important products include sugarcane, grapes, corn, wheat, and machinery. Although many South Africans are poor, most South Africans have clean drinking water and electricity.

recipe for 'kerrievis' [pickled fish]. . . . Often served as a first course, pickled fish is served as the main course with a salad of potato and accompanied by some dressed lettuce leaves."[3]

Meat and Wild Game

Meat is another essential part of South Africans' diets. South African tribal people have been raising cattle and sheep for centuries. When European settlers ar-

South Africans enjoy the meat of wild game, including springbok, which is a type of gazelle.

rived in the 16th century, they established cattle and sheep ranches. Wild game is also abundant. **Springbok** is a type of gazelle that has been hunted for meat in South Africa since early times. It is especially popular. So is a wild deer called **gembok**. These animals eat native grasses and herbs, which gives their meat a fresh, natural taste. South African professor Leatita Radder explains: "The animals roam freely in their natural habitat. . . . [The meat] is free of synthetic hormones and the influence of pollution, thus making it a natural and healthy product."[4]

South Africans eat meat as often as possible. They grill, roast, fry, and stew it. They fill savory pies with it. They dry it, turning it into biltong—spicy, salty meat strips similar to jerky. It is a favorite snack and sandwich food. South Africans also make many varieties of boerewors (BER-uh-vors), or sausages, which they grill or fry.

Indeed, at any given time, foods like boerewors and other meats, mealies, vegetables, and fish and seafood can be found cooking somewhere in South Africa. These ingredients help connect the people of this diverse land.

The Rainbow Nation

South Africa is nicknamed the Rainbow Nation. People from more than thirty ethnic groups call South Africa their home. These include: African tribal people like the **Zulu** and **Xhosa** (KHO-suh); Dutch, German, and other European settlers who became known as **Afrikaners** (af-rih-KAHN-ers); British, Indonesian, and Indian people; and people of mixed-race ancestry.

Between 1948 and 1994 South Africa had a political system known as **apartheid** (uh-PAR-tight). The apartheid government separated people by race and gave privileges to white South Africans. Apartheid caused anger and conflict. It kept South Africa's different ethnic groups from getting to know each other.

South Africa's People

Hunter-gatherers known as the San were among South Africa's earliest people. San descendants still live in South Africa. They speak an unusual language that includes clicking sounds.

About 1,500 years ago Bantu-speaking groups began migrating from northern Africa to South Africa. These groups were the ancestors of the Zulu, Xhosa, Ndebele, and Swazi people. They were farmers and cattle herders. The Zulu, who make up the largest ethnic group in South Africa today, were fierce warriors.

Portuguese seamen first made contact with South Africans in 1498. In 1647 the Dutch colonized Cape Town. The colony served as a stopping-off point for Dutch ships traveling between Europe and Indonesia. Soon, Dutch, German, and French settlers arrived. This group became known as Afrikaners, or Boers. They brought slaves and servants from Indonesia, Malaysia, and India with them. The British ruled South Africa in the late 1700s.

Apartheid is now a thing of the past. Modern South Africans enjoy sharing their distinct cultures. Their meals, too, blend the cooking styles and favorite ingredients of the many groups that are a part of South Africa. One South African chef, Bill Gallagher, puts it this way: "As South Africa becomes more united, as the people mix and match and work together, we … see the emergence of [what] … we would like to call Rainbow Cuisine, using, as it does, all the different ingredients and influences to create a melting pot of flavors."[5]

South Africa's National Dish

Bobotie (BOO-boot) is South Africa's national dish. It is a casserole that contains minced meat mixed with spices, onions, dried fruit, lemon juice, and apricot preserves. The meat is covered with an egg sauce and baked until the flavors blend and the ingredients are tender.

South Africans have been eating bobotie since the 17th century. Indonesian slaves who were brought to Cape Town by the Dutch created the dish. They changed the recipes that they brought from their homeland to suit their new environment and the tastes of their masters. The dishes they created became known as **Cape Malay cooking**. In making bobotie, the slaves used Indonesian spices like ginger and bitter yellow turmeric (TER-muh-rik). They added the Dutch favorite of finely ground meat, the Afrikaner specialty of apricot preserves, and a custard-like egg topping similar to toppings used

Bobotie, a casserole of minced meat, spices, onions, and preserves covered with an egg sauce, is South Africa's national dish.

Yellow Rice

Bredies and bobotie are often served with yellow rice. The rice gets its color from a golden spice called turmeric.

Ingredients
1 cup rice
2 cups water
¼ cup raisins
½ teaspoon turmeric
2 tablespoons sugar
2 tablespoons butter

Instructions
1. Bring the water to a boil.
2. Stir in all the other ingredients.
3. Reduce the heat to low. Cover the pot.
4. Cook until the rice is fluffy and the water has evaporated, about twenty minutes.

Serves 4.

Yellow rice is served along with many South African dishes.

in many British dishes.

The dish has a creamy texture and a fruity aroma. It tastes sweet and savory at the same time, which is a combination that South Africans love. Bobotie is usually served with sliced bananas and yellow rice. Turmeric makes the rice yellow and spicy, while raisins and sugar make it sweet. Bobotie, according to Michael Olivier, "is probably the most widely known and loved of all Cape dishes."[6]

Bredies

Bredies (BREE-eds) are other local favorites. Bredies are hearty stews that contain lamb and a vegetable. No one knows where bredies originated. Some historians think the stews were created by South Africa's Xhosa or Zulu people, who have been making a variety of stews for thousands of years. Others trace the stews' beginnings to Afrikaner farmers. Still others claim that since bredies are flavored with the common Indonesian ingredients of ginger, cinnamon, cloves, and chili peppers, they must have been invented by Indonesian cooks. Most likely, all of these groups together contributed to bredies' development.

There are many varieties of bredies. All are named for the type of vegetable used in that particular stew. Early bredies usually contained wild greens, such as waterblommetjies, or native vegetables, like pumpkin. Afrikaner farmers introduced other vegetables to South Africa, like cauliflower and cabbage. These were soon added to bredies, too.

No matter the type of vegetable added, all bredies are cooked slowly until the meat is meltingly tender and all the flavors combine. In the past bredies were made in heavy cast-iron pots over hot coals. The pots were given to European settlers when they arrived in Cape Town. Today, bredies are cooked on stove tops or in slow cookers. Fattier cuts of meat are preferred, because they add rich flavor to the stew. Onions, garlic, and potatoes thicken the dish and give it an earthy aroma.

South Africans eat bredies often but because there are so many varieties, South Africans do not get tired of the dish. "We ate a lot of bredies when I was a child," recalls Magdaleen Van Wyk. "Tomato bredie was usually served on a Monday, with cooked rice and a green salad. … We always called … [green bean bredie] Thursday bredie, because that's the day my mother made it."[7]

Bredies are flavorful stews that can feature any of a number of vegetables as well as meat, greens, onions, garlic, and potatoes.

Green Bean Bredie

Fresh or thawed frozen green beans can be used. Broth can be substituted for water.

Ingredients
2 pounds stewing lamb, cut into cubes
1 cup water
2 onions, peeled and sliced
1½ pounds green beans, ends cut off, sliced
2 large potatoes, peeled and cut into chunks
2 tablespoons butter or oil
½ teaspoon each salt, pepper, thyme, garlic

Instructions
1. Heat the butter or oil in a stew pot over medium heat. Add the onions and meat. Cook until the meat is browned on all sides.
2. Combine the water and spices. Pour this mixture over the meat and onions. Reduce the heat to low. Cover the pot. Cook for one hour.
3. Add the beans and potatoes. Cover the pot. Cook on low until the vegetables are soft.

Serve over rice. Serves 4–6.

Curry

Curry is another South African favorite. It was first made in India, where the term *curry* describes any number of stew-like dishes in which meat, chicken, fish, seafood, or vegetables are cooked in a spicy sauce. Indian servants who worked on Afrikaner sugar planta-

A cook pours fish curry into a bread bowl to make bunny chow, which is considered South Africa's earliest fast food.

tions brought curry to South Africa. According to author Hilary Biller, the Indian servants "brought with them a food culture that was to have a tremendous impact on palates [taste in food] countrywide."[8]

In the past, some South Africans refused to eat curry. They considered it servants' food. However, Nobel

Peace Prize–winner Nelson Mandela did not share this point of view. Mandela was a leader of South Africa's anti-apartheid movement, which believed in equality for all South Africans. He also was the first South African president elected in a multi-racial election. Mandela often ate vegetable curry at dinners in which members of the anti-apartheid movement met. Not only did he like the taste, he felt that eating curry was a symbol of the cross-cultural freedom he was working for. "This vegetable curry," Mandela wrote in his autobiography, "reminds us of the importance of opening our minds (and our taste buds) to people and flavors that may be unfamiliar."[9] So in a way, the modern South African government was formed over curry dinners.

Today, curry is eaten by almost all South Africans. It is made with snoek, shrimp, crabs, lamb, beef, chicken, pork, or vegetables. Ground spices such as turmeric, cumin, and garlic mixed with liquid form the sauce and give the curry its zesty flavor. The ingredients and level of spiciness vary throughout the country. Curries made in the city of Durban are the hottest. Outside of India, Durban has the largest population of Indians in the world. It was there that bunny chow, a favorite type of South African curry, was invented.

Bunny chow is South Africa's earliest fast food. It was created so Indian servants could eat in the fields long before paper plates were invented. To make it, cooks hollow out the center of a half loaf of unsliced bread, creating a bowl that is then filled with curry. The bread that was removed is placed on top. It serves as both a lid and a dunking tool. The bread absorbs the spicy sauce and becomes moist, soft, and delicious. When the curry is gone, the bread bowl is eaten. Writer Wanda Hennig says, "We'd go to the grubby little harbor take-out … and order 'a bunny.' . . . We'd get half a loaf of soft white bread filled with a lethal bean curry that made your eyes water. . . . You'd eat it with your fingers, dunking and dipping and chewing and licking."[10]

Sunday Lunch

Roasted meat is another favorite dish. The custom of serving it for Sunday lunch was brought to South Africa by the British. Afrikaner farmers adopted it and turned it into a weekly family feast featuring home-raised beef, lamb, or chicken. The meat was served with a huge variety of hefty side dishes known as boerekos (BER-uh-kohs), or farmer's food. Green beans, yams, pumpkins, pap, salads, pickled vegetables, and sweet and savory puddings were just a few of the popular side dishes. South African writer Alida Ryder explains: "Our Sundays always involved us going to church in the mornings followed by a

A plate of traditional South African Sunday lunch foods includes roasted meat, potatoes, and vegetable sides.

Mopane Worms

Mopane worms are considered a special food by many South Africans. The creatures are not worms at all, but rather large spiky green-and-blue caterpillars. They live in mopane trees, which are trees with butterfly-shaped leaves that grow only in Africa. Harvesters, who are often women and children, pick the worms out of the trees by hand. Then they squeeze the creatures' tails to crush their internal organs and to force out a part of the animal that is not good to eat.

The worms are rarely eaten fresh. Instead, they are preserved by being dried in the sun, smoked, or pickled. Pickled mopane worms are sold in South African markets. Dried worms are eaten as a crispy snack. The dried worms are also rehydrated by soaking them in water until they are plump. Then they are fried or added to stews.

Raising, harvesting, and processing mopane worms is an important business in South Africa.

Dried mopane worms are eaten as a snack in South Africa.

family lunch. As you walked through the front door the smell of onions and green beans cooking, leg of lamb roasting, and sweet potato or pumpkin would welcome you."[11]

Most modern South Africans no longer raise the food they serve for Sunday lunch. But getting together for a midday meal on Sunday is still part of South African life and tradition. So are favorite dishes like curry, bredies, and bobotie. These foods reflect the different groups that have made South Africa a rainbow nation.

Favorite Treats

South Africans enjoy many tasty treats for snacks and desserts. **Rooibos** (ROY-boss) **tea**, sweet fruit-based delicacies, custard pies known as melkterts, and fried pastries called koeksisters (COOK-sis-ters) are local favorites.

Red Tea

South Africans love tea. Rooibos, or red bush tea, is an herbal tea that comes from a plant that grows only in the mountains of South Africa. It is the top choice of South Africans. They sip it hot or iced with milk and sugar, day and night. South Africans say the tea soothes them and improves their health. They are probably right. Rooibos tea contains no caffeine or other in-

Rooibos bushes, which grow only in the mountains of South Africa, make a healthful, delicious tea that is sold throughout the country.

gredients that boost energy. It does, however, contain vitamin C, several minerals, and **antioxidants**, which strengthen the immune system and help the body fight disease. Other substances in the tea appear to have properties that reduce indigestion and anxious feelings. South Africans so believe in the tea's benefits that the herb used to make it is added to baby food.

Although South Africa's tribal people have been drinking the tea for centuries to treat or prevent illness, it did not become popular with other South Africans until World War II, in the 1940s. At that time black tea imported from Asia was in short supply. As a replacement, South Africans turned to rooibos tea. They fell in love with its distinctive dark-red color, honey-like scent, and sweet, nutty flavor. As a result, rooibos tea has become South Africa's unofficial national drink.

The tea pairs well with a variety of flavors and these flavors are added to rooibos tea and sold everywhere. Orange-cinnamon, vanilla, mint, and spiced apple are just a few popular flavors of the drink. Rooibos latte (LAH-tay), hot tea topped with steamed milk, is another favorite. South Africans like the scent and flavor of the tea so much that rooibus extract is also used in perfumes and cosmetics, and to flavor ice cream, yogurt, and stews.

Kruger National Park

Kruger National Park was founded as a wildlife refuge in 1898 by the government of South Africa. It covers 7,523 square miles (19,485km), and is one of the largest parks in the world. It contains 147 species of mammals, 507 species of birds, 116 species of reptiles, 34 species of amphibians, and 49 species of fish.

All of the animals roam freely. There are no fences separating the animals from park visitors. White rhinos, lions, leopards, cheetahs, monkeys, baboons, elephants, giraffes, hippos, zebras, buffalo, eagles, herons, storks, vultures, and crocodiles are just some of the resident wildlife.

Nearly 1 million people visit the park each year. Many South African families return annually. Visitors can stay overnight in rest camps and lodges. They can take either guided walking safaris or driving tours.

Iced Rooibos Tea

Rooibos tea is sold in most American supermarkets under the name red tea or red bush tea.

Ingredients
4 rooibos teabags
½ gallon boiling water
½ lemon, sliced
10 mint leaves
ice cubes
sugar or honey to taste

Instructions
1. Put the tea bags, mint, lemon slices, and sugar in a large pitcher or container. Pour in the boiling water and stir well. Let the mixture steep and cool.
2. Remove the tea bags. Stir. Refrigerate.
3. Put some ice cubes in a glass. Pour the tea through a strainer into the glass.

Serves 6.

Hot or iced tea can be made from the dried leaves of the rooibos bush.

Fruit Treats

A cup of rooibos tea is usually drunk with sweet, fruity treats. South Africa's mild climate and fertile soil make it easy to grow a wide range of delicious fruits. In the past, Afrikaner farmers planted fruit trees wherever they settled. Today fruit growing is a major South African industry. "We can choose from the most tropical, large, fleshy mangoes, to the finest berries—even delicate raspberries are there for the taking during the course of the year,"[12] explains South African chef Shirley Guy.

Fruit is grown all over South Africa. Some South African fruits, like grapefruit, cherries, watermelons, plums, pineapples, grapes, mangoes, nectarines, apricots, bananas, and peaches, are well-known to North Americans. Others, such as tangerine-like fruits called naartjes (NAR-chees) and sour, yellow, pear-shaped quinces (KWINT-sess), are less common to North Americans.

South Africans use fruit to make pies, tarts, cakes, candies, and preserves. Sweets made with dried fruits are very popular. A fruit roll is one such treat. To make a fruit roll, cooks mix cut fruit with sugar. Any type of fruit can be used. Plump, juicy apricots, peaches, and plums are favorites. The cut fruit is spread onto a baking pan that is covered with nylon netting to keep out insects. Then it is set out in the sun to dry. Once it is dried, more sugar is drizzled on top. The sweet, chewy confection is rolled into a cylinder and cut into pieces.

Savory Snacks

South Africans enjoy savory snacks almost as much as sweet ones. A gatsby is a favorite. It is a submarine sandwich made on a long roll and topped with so many different foods that it is like a multi-course meal. The roll is stuffed with a choice of fillings, such as fish, chicken, lamb, steak, octopus, or sausage. Hot fried potatoes top the meat or fish. Salad, pickles, and a variety of sauces come next. The sandwich is usually cut into four sections. It is so big and hearty that it is usually shared by two to four people.

Samosas are another popular treat. Samosas are fried pastry triangles filled with meat, vegetables, or potatoes mixed with spices. They were introduced to South Africa by Indian immigrants. Samosas taste light and delicate. They are usually served with a fruity chutney sauce or a sambal chili sauce.

Samosas are fried pastries filled with spiced meat, vegetables, or potatoes.

"Fruit rolls," explains author Harva Hachten, "utilize [use] the many fruits grown in the hospitable [pleasant] southern climate. The recipe also highlights the hot, dry atmospheric conditions prevalent in vast areas of South Africa, for it is 'cooked' outdoors by the heat of the sun."[13]

Konfyt (KON-fate) is another popular fruit treat. It is a sweet, jellylike fruit preserve that South Africans make by boiling large chunks of fruit in sugary syrup seasoned with ginger and cinnamon. They eat konfyt by the spoonful, much like pudding or flavored gelatin, or they spread it onto muffins, scones, and warm bread. Konfyt is also served as a dessert along with cheese or ice cream. Konfyt can be made with almost any fruit, including water-melon rind. Slightly sour fruits taste especially good. Their tartness gives balance to the sugary, warmly spiced syrup.

In the past, making konfyt was a big part of most South African cooks'

A country store in South Africa offers various kinds of konfyt, a type of fruit preserve that is served as a spread or with dessert.

lives. When fruit was harvested, homemakers made jar after jar of konfyt as a way to preserve the bounty for future use. Today most South Africans buy ready-made konfyt in supermarkets. Still, some South Africans like to make their own. South African blogger Jolisa Grobler explains: "Making preserves … were such a big part of our lives growing up. A huge chunk of my childhood memories consist of us, sitting around a table in our or my grandmothers' kitchens peeling, boiling, tasting and eating. . . . My mother continues the tradition and I hope to fill her shoes one day too."[14]

Melktert

Melktert, a soft, moist custard pie, is another traditional sweet. It was brought to South Africa by Dutch settlers. It makes use of the abundance of milk, butter, and eggs produced on South African farms.

Melktert is similar in texture to a vanilla cream pie, but moister and creamier. It begins with a rich puff pastry crust. The crust is filled with sweet, light custard made from a mixture of milk, eggs, sugar, cinnamon, and butter. Some cooks add bits of dried naartjies, almond extract, and coconut milk to the custard. These ingredients add an enchanting tropical flavor and aroma.

Melktert is a favorite dessert to have with tea. According to authors Magdaleen Van Wyk and Pat Barton, melktert "has to be the most famous South African sweet tart. . . . It's a sublime taste experience."[15]

Melktert is a creamy custard pie that is often served with tea.

Sizzling Cake

Koeksisters are pastries similar to doughnuts or crullers. They are another popular dessert and snack. Koeksisters are fried. In fact, the word *koeksister* means "sizzling cake" in Afrikaner. And, the pastries do sizzle when they are dropped into hot oil.

Both South Africa's Afrikaner and Indonesian people claim koeksisters as their own. To make the pastries, cooks braid strips of pastry dough and then deep

Melktert

This is an easy melktert recipe. Be sure it is completely set before eating.

Ingredients
1 graham-cracker piecrust
2 cups milk
1 tablespoon unsalted butter
1½ tablespoons flour
1 tablespoon cornstarch
½ cup sugar
1 egg
2 teaspoons cinnamon, divided
1 teaspoon vanilla

Instructions
1. Boil the milk, butter, and 1 teaspoon cinnamon.
2. Mix all the other ingredients except the remaining cinnamon together. Add the mixture to the milk. Reduce the heat to medium low and cook until the mixture thickens (for about five minutes), stirring often.
3. Fill the piecrust with the milk mixture. Sprinkle with the remaining 1 teaspoon cinnamon. Refrigerate overnight.

Makes one pie. Serves 8.

fry them until they are golden. As soon as the pastries are pulled from the frying pan, they are dipped in ice-cold syrup made with sugar, lemon juice, ginger, and cinnamon. The syrup coats the pastries with a layer of crispy, sweet, sticky goodness. With their sweet, fried taste, their candy-like icing, and their warm, cit-

Koeksisters are a sweet fried pastry glazed with a tasty syrup.

rusy fragrance, koeksisters are hard to resist. According to South African author Michael Tracey, the fried treats are a

> mainstream munch, eaten as a sweet snack, at braaivleis [barbecues], sporting events, cocktail parties, in fact you'll find koeksisters popping up almost everywhere. ... Koeksisters are a favorite of all South Africans who have a sweet tooth. People sell them outside shopping malls to earn an income. You will find them at all fund raising functions where food is sold. If you like sweet things you will certainly enjoy these. But be careful, they're so nice that it's easy to over indulge.[16]

South Africans do enjoy sweets. Whether as snacks or desserts, treats like koeksisters, melkterts, fruit rolls, and konfyt accompanied by a relaxing cup of rooibos tea are a delightful way to satisfy a sweet tooth.

Chapter 4

Celebrating the South African Way

South Africa is blessed with a warm, mild climate. It is a perfect place to enjoy outdoor activities. South African celebrations are as likely to be held outdoors as indoors. But no matter where celebrations are held, special food is always part of the festivities.

Braais

When family and friends get together in South Africa to celebrate birthdays, anniversaries, or just for fun, chances are the festivities will center around a **braai** (bry), or barbecue. Cooking over an open fire has been a South African tradition for centuries. In fact, it was the usual cooking method of South Africa's early tribal people and of the Voortrekkers. Voortrekkers were Afri-

Diners at a lodge enjoy a braai, an outdoor meal cooked over a fire that is a popular way for South Africans to socialize or celebrate special occasions.

kaner farmers who ventured in ox-drawn wagons from Cape Town into the inland areas of South Africa.

What began as a necessity for South Africa's early people has become a part of South African culture. In fact, almost every South African attends a braai on September 24th, which is National Braai Day. South

Braai Bread

Bread made on a braai grill is often part of South African festivities. The bread known as roosterkoek (ROOR-stir-cook) is a traditional bread similar to pancakes that South Africans have been making over an open fire for centuries. To make it, cooks prepare dough by mixing yeast, flour, water, eggs, and butter. After the dough rises, it is formed into little patties that are placed directly onto the braai grill. The dough must be thick and stiff. Otherwise, it will slide through the grill holes.

The bread is flipped like hamburgers. It is done cooking when both sides are golden brown. It is eaten right off the braai, while the bread is still warm. The patties are split open like buns and spread with butter.

When South Africans go camping they make roosterkoek by wrapping the dough around long sticks, which they hold over the campfire.

Africans, however, do not wait for National Braai Day to barbecue. Most have a braai at least once a week. According to an article on the South African cooking website eJozi's Recipe Book, "South Africans won't easily let anything get in the way of a good braai, not even the weather. Come rain or sunshine (fortunately it's mostly sunshine), they just love it. For us a braai is much more than just a way of cooking, it has become a way of life."[17]

Parks, picnic grounds, beaches, and backyards are all good locations for a braai. Typically, the host builds the fire out of aromatic hardwoods and does the cooking. The male guests gather around the fire to help. This gathering is part of the celebration, since the men snack, drink, and visit as they work. The women talk with each other as they prepare the side dishes, which usually include pap, various salads, bread, and desserts.

Skewered Meat

Braai menus vary. Steaks, lamb chops, fish, chicken, and sausages are all standard fare. A popular dish called

Having Fun in South Africa

Soccer, or football, as it is known in South Africa, is the most popular sport in the nation. South Africans love to play soccer, and they love to watch teams like the national team Bafana Bafana play. South Africans were proud to host the FIFA World Cup championship in 2010. The games were played in ten stadiums in nine host cities across South Africa.

Other popular sports are cricket and rugby. These games were brought to South Africa by the British. Golf is another favorite sport. So are other mild-climate sports like swimming, surfing, tennis, rock climbing, hiking, hang gliding, and bungee jumping. Running in long distance races is another popular pastime. About 13,000 runners compete in the annual Comrades Marathon, a race that covers about 56 miles (90km). Long-distance bicycle and canoe races are common, too.

sosaties (suh-SAH-tees) is made with spicy skewered meat. The dish was brought to South Africa by Indonesian cooks.

To make it, cooks first marinate chunks of lamb in a slightly sweet, slightly sour, slightly spicy sauce for hours, or even days. Soaking in the sauce tenderizes, perfumes, and flavors the meat. The ingredients in sosaties vary from cook to cook. Many have their own secret recipes. Curry powder, apricot jam, lemon juice, and garlic are common ingredients. "Each South African cook has her own special recipe for sosaties," explains Hachten, "and the spice proportions can be varied endlessly. Some prefer lemon juice to vinegar

Sosaties are tasty skewers of marinated meat and apricots grilled over hot coals.

Sosaties

Sosaties are usually made with lamb, but beef or chicken can be substituted. If wood skewers are used they should be soaked in water overnight. Sosaties can be cooked on a grill or in a broiler.

Ingredients
1 pound lamb, cut into 2-inch cubes
½ cup dried apricots
2 tablespoons vegetable oil
1 onion, chopped
1 tablespoon curry powder
½ cup white wine vinegar
½ cup water
1 tablespoon apricot jam
1 tablespoon brown sugar
1 teaspoon garlic powder
1 tablespoon flour or cornmeal

Instructions
1. Heat the oil in a large pan. Fry the onion until it becomes clear.
2. Add all the other ingredients except the apricots and lamb. Cook for about five minutes over low heat, stirring constantly.
3. Put the apricots and lamb in a large bowl. Pour the sauce on the meat and lamb. Cover with foil or plastic wrap. Refrigerate overnight.
4. Thread the lamb and apricots alternately on thin skewers. Grill the meat on a grill or in a broiler. When the meat browns on one side, turn the skewer over. The meat is done when it is brown on both sides and pinkish-brown inside.

Serves 4.

and many won't make sosaties unless they can get **tamarind** leaves—a Malay [Indonesian] ingredient that imparts the sour note in the sweet-sour dish."[18]

On the day of the braai, the meat is threaded through thin skewers, alternating with dried apricots, and grilled over hot coals. The apricots add a fruity taste and aroma to the dish. When the meat is brown on the outside and soft and juicy within, it is ready to eat. It tastes tangy, smoky, and pleasantly spicy, and it is so soft and moist it can be cut with a spoon.

Potjies

Potjies (POY-kees) are another braai favorite. A potjie is a stew that is cooked in a special round-bottomed, three-legged pot that is placed directly on hot coals. A potjie can contain almost anything, including fish, beef, chicken, oxtail, springbok, and mutton, which is meat from sheep. Every cook has his or her own way of making a potjie. For example, one cook might make fish potjie with tuna fish, mussels, hot and sweet peppers, spices, and onions, while another will use snoek, potatoes, carrots, and spices. Some cooks add beer to beef potjie, and some add bananas to oxtail potjie. The cook makes the dish exactly how he or she likes it.

South Africans take potjie making very seriously. Potjie competitions are favorite events at South African fairs. According to Peter Thomas, a South African cook and author, "The preparing of a potjie meal is very much an individual thing with every aspiring cook experimenting to come up with the 'perfect' potjie, then

A special three-legged pot placed directly on hot coals is used to cook potjies, a type of stew enjoyed at braais in South Africa.

enter it in a potjie cookoff and just maybe, walk off with the first prize!"[19]

It takes patience to make a perfect potjie. Potjies are cooked in layers. First come the meat or fish and onions. They are cooked until they are almost done. Then, layers of vegetables are added. Finally, liquid or sauce is poured into the pot. The whole thing is left to simmer for hours until the liquid thickens and the ingredients are buttery soft. Celebrants do not mind the wait. They nibble on side dishes while they visit with each other. "Time should be of no consequence,"

Trifle

Trifle is easy to make. You can use any type of yellow or white cake and any type of cookies, and fruit. Trifle is usually served in a glass bowl.

Ingredients
1 unfrosted yellow cake, cut into large cubes
1 package (3 ounces) instant vanilla pudding, prepared and cooled
8 ounces frozen whipped topping, thawed
1 cup crushed almonds
1 cup gingersnaps, crushed
1 cup canned or fresh peaches, cut into chunks

Instructions
1. Put a layer of the cake on the bottom of a large serving bowl.
2. Spread a layer of pudding on the cake. Top with a layer of nuts, a layer of cookies, a layer of the peaches, and another layer of cake. Spread the whipped cream on top of the cake.

Chill before serving. Serves 6–8.

A trifle, which is a layered dessert featuring cake or cookies, fruit, and whipped cream, is especially popular around the Christmas holidays.

Thomas explains. "The beauty of preparing potjiekos [potjies] is that it gives you time to sip your favorite drink and enjoy chatting to your guests while sitting round a friendly fire."[20]

Christmas in the Summer

Other celebrations revolve around holidays. Christmas, in particular, is a joyous time in South Africa. Since South Africa is in the southern hemisphere, the month of Christmas, December, falls in the middle of the summer. Many South Africans like to eat Christmas dinner outdoors. Others prefer to celebrate indoors.

The main course varies. It may be braaied or cooked indoors. Spit-roasted pig, turkey, or roast beef are all popular choices. No matter what else is served, traditional Christmas desserts like trifles and Christmas pudding that were brought to South Africa by the British are usually part of the meal. A trifle is a rich multi-layered mixture that begins with sweet, soft sponge cake. A thick delectable layer of homemade custard tops the cake. A sprinkle of nuts comes next, topped by crumbled cookies, and fresh or dried fruit. The whole thing is crowned with an airy mound of whipped cream and a bright-red candied cherry. "Christmas wouldn't be Christmas without a trifle,"[21] insist authors Magdaleen Van Wyk and Pat Barton.

Christmas pudding is another holiday favorite. It looks and tastes more like a moist cake than a creamy pudding. Making it takes time, which is why many South Africans buy it ready-made right before Christ-

Flaming brandy is ladled over Christmas pudding, a common holiday treat in South Africa.

mas. Those who make it themselves usually begin four Sundays before Christmas on a day known as Stir Up Sunday. The day gets its name because it is the custom for every family member to stir the pudding as it cooks while making a Christmas wish. Adding to the fun, little charms of reindeer, angels, and other Christmas symbols, are put into the pudding for the children to find when they eat the dessert.

The pudding is made with candied fruits, sugar, butter, nuts, eggs, flour, and spices. The mixture is poured into a special cloth bag, which is placed in a pot of boiling water and steamed for hours. When the pudding is done, it is stored in a cool place until Christmas. This gives the different flavors plenty of time to blend together and become stronger. Before it is served, the pudding is steamed again. Brandy, an alcoholic beverage, is poured over the top and set afire. Then, much to everyone's excitement, the flaming pudding is brought to the table.

South African celebrations are full of fun. Whether they are held indoors or outdoors, special foods like Christmas pudding, trifle, sosaties, and potjie help make every celebration memorable.

Mass (weight)

1 ounce (oz.)	= 28.0 grams (g)
8 ounces	= 227.0 grams
1 pound (lb.) or 16 ounces	= 0.45 kilograms (kg)
2.2 pounds	= 1.0 kilogram

Liquid Volume

1 teaspoon (tsp.)	= 5.0 milliliters (ml)
1 tablespoon (tbsp.)	= 15.0 milliliters
1 fluid ounce (oz.)	= 30.0 milliliters
1 cup (c.)	= 240 milliliters
1 pint (pt.)	= 480 milliliters
1 quart (qt.)	= 0.96 liters (l)
1 gallon (gal.)	= 3.84 liters

Pan Sizes

8-inch cake pan	= 20 x 4-centimeter cake pan
9-inch cake pan	= 23 x 3.5-centimeter cake pan
11 x 7-inch baking pan	= 28 x 18-centimeter baking pan
13 x 9-inch baking pan	= 32.5 x 23-centimeter baking pan
9 x 5-inch loaf pan	= 23 x 13-centimeter loaf pan
2-quart casserole	= 2-liter casserole

Temperature

212°F	= 100°C (boiling point of water)
225°F	= 110°C
250°F	= 120°C
275°F	= 135°C
300°F	= 150°C
325°F	= 160°C
350°F	= 180°C
375°F	= 190°C
400°F	= 200°C

Length

1/4 inch (in.)	= 0.6 centimeters (cm)
1/2 inch	= 1.25 centimeters
1 inch	= 2.5 centimeters

Notes

Chapter 1: A Land of Contrasts

1. Thuli. "Umphokoqo—A Dish Fit for a President." Mzansi Style Cuisine, February 28, 2011. www.mzansistylecuisine.co.za/?p=12.

2. Magdaleen Van Wyk and Pat Barton. *Traditional South African Cooking.* Cape Town, South Africa: Random House Struik, 2007. p. 30.

3. Michael Oliver. "Pickled Fish, Kerrievis." *Michael Olivier*, June, 29, 2009. www.michaelolivier.co.za/2009/06/29/pickled-fish-kerrievis.

4. Quoted in Gwynne Conlyn. *Delicious Travel.* Johannesburg, South Africa: Jacana Media, 2004, p. 164.

Chapter 2: The Rainbow Nation

5. Quoted in Hilary Biller and John Peacock. *Tastes: Thoughts on South African Cuisine.* Halfway House, South Africa: Zebra, 1998, p. 70.

6. Michael Olivier. "Bobotie—A Classical Cape Dish." *Michael Olivier*, June 15, 2009. http://michaelolivier.co.za/2009/06/15/376/.

7. Van Wyk and Barton. *Traditional South African Cooking,* p. 51.

8. Biller and Peacock. *Tastes: Thoughts on South African Cuisine,* p. 55.

9. Quoted in Elizabeth Alpern. "Foods of Freedom: South African Vegetable Curry." *The Jew and the Carrot*, April 12, 2011. http://blogs.forward.com/the-jew-and-the-carrot/136936/.

10. Wanda Hennig. "What You Need to Know About Bunny Chow When You Visit Durban, South Africa." Examiner.com, May 31, 2010. www.examiner.com/culinary-travel-in-san-francisco/what-you-need-to-know-about-bunny-chow-when-you-visit-durban-south-africa.

11. Alida Ryder. "South African Malva Pudding and Memories of Sunday Lunches." *Honest Cooking*, March 14, 2011. http://honestcooking.com/2011/03/14/south-african-malva-pudding-and-memories-of-sunday-lunches/.

Chapter 3: Favorite Treats

12. Quoted in Biller and Peacock. *Tastes: Thoughts on South African Cuisine*, p. 77.
13. Harva Hachten. *Best of Regional African Cooking*. New York: Hippocrene, 1970, p. 194.
14. Jolisa Grobler. "Nostalgia with Makataan Konfyt (watermelon preserve)." *Orchid Chef*, March 13, 2011. http://orchidchef.blogspot.com/2011/03/nostalgia-with-makataan-konfyt.html.
15. Van Wyk and Barton. *Traditional South African Cooking*, p. 101.
16. Michael Tracey. "Koeksisters," *Afri Chef*. www.africhef.com/Koeksisters-Recipe.html.

Chapter 4: Celebrating the South African Way

17. "Braai in South African Cuisine," *eJozi's Recipe Book*. www.ejozi.co.za/south-african-cuisine/braai.html.
18. Hachten. *Best of Regional African Cooking*, p. 134.
19. Peter Thomas. "My Potjiekos Page," *Funky Munky*. http://funkymunky.co.za/potjiekos.html.
20. Thomas. "My Potjiekos Page."
21. Van Wyk and Barton. *Traditional South African Cooking*, p. 81.

Glossary

Afrikaners: South Africans of Dutch, German, and French origin.

antioxidants: Substances that strengthen the immune system and fight disease.

apartheid: Former South African political system that separated people by race and gave privileges to white South Africans.

bobotie: A minced-meat casserole that is South Africa's national dish.

braai: A barbecue; also the act of barbecuing

Cape Malay cooking: A style of cooking created by Indonesians in Cape Town, South Africa, that mixes Indonesian and European cooking styles.

gembok: A wild antelope that is hunted for food in South Africa.

mealie: South African term for corn.

mealie meal: South African term for cornmeal.

pap: A porridge-like food made with cornmeal.

rooibos tea: An herbal tea that grows on a plant found only in South Africa.

samp: Coarsely pounded dry corn kernels.

snoek: A saltwater fish that is very popular in South Africa.

springbok: A wild gazelle that is hunted for meat in South Africa.

tamarind: A tart tropical fruit.

Xhosa: A black South African ethnic group.

Zulu: The largest black South African ethnic group.

Books

Melissa Koosmann. *Meet Our New Student from South Africa.* Hockessin, DE: Mitchell Lane, 2009. Information about South Africa's culture, geography, and history with craft projects.

Melissa Koosmann. *The Fall of Apartheid in South Africa.* Hockessin, DE: Mitchell Lane, 2009. Looks at what apartheid was, the resistance movement to end apartheid, and the heroic people involved in the movement.

Claire Thorp. *South Africa.* Chicago: Heinemann, 2010. Information about South Africa including its geography, climate, people, history, and government.

Chris Ward. *Discover South Africa.* New York: PowerKids, 2010. Looks at South Africa's geography, people, culture, and economics with photos, maps, and charts.

Websites

Kids Around the World, "Africa,"(www.katw.org/pages/sitepage.cfm?id=55). This African page links to a wealth of information about the South African flag, South African daily life and culture, maps, and an interview with a South African child.

National Geographic Kids, "Find People & Places, South Africa" (http://kids.nationalgeographic.com/kids/places/find/south-africa/). This website displays information about South Africa, beautiful photos, a picture of the flag, a map, and an e-card.

PBS, "Africa for Kids, My World" (http://pbskids.org/africa/myworld/ngaka.html). Photos with brief descriptions about life in South Africa is presented by a group of South African students.

Time for Kids, "South Africa" (www.timeforkids.com/TFK/teachers/aw/wr/main/0%2C28132%2C590829%2C00.html). Lots of information about South Africa, including a fact file, timeline, and sightseeing guide with an interactive map and pictures.

Index

Picture Credits

Cover photo: © Rua Castilho/The Food Passionates/Corbis

Abraham Badenhorst/Shutterstock.com, 47

© AfriPics.com/Alamy, 27

Anke van Wyk/Shutterstock.com, 26

© Bon Appetit/Alamy, 15, 34, 37

Christopher Elwell/Shutterstock.com, 50

Elzbieta Sekowska/Shutterstock.com, 10

© Food Centrale Hamburg GmbH/Alamy, 44

© Foodfotos/Alamy, 39

© foodimagecollection/Alamy, 48

© frans lemmens/Alamy, 35

Gale, Cengage Learning, 5

© John Warburton-Lee Photography/Alamy, 41

kiboka/Shutterstock.com, 32

© Matt Rearden/Alamy, 30

© Profimedia International s.r.o./Alamy, 24

© Steve Cavalier/Alamy, 11

© Suretha Rous/Alamy, 13

© Tim Hill/Alamy, 19, 22

© Tom Tracy Photography/Alamy, 20

© vario images GmbH & Co.KG/Alamy, 6

About the Author

Barbara Sheen is the author of more than 70 books for young people. She lives in New Mexico with her family. In her spare time, she likes to swim, walk, garden, and read. Of course, she loves to cook!